THE BIBLE, THE ~~~~~~~~~~,

SEVENTH-DAY ADVENTISM

or

Is Seventh-day Adventism Evangelical?

BY

GORDON R. LEWIS

PRESBYTERIAN AND REFORMED PUBLISHING CO.
PHILLIPSBURG, NEW JERSEY

Printed in the United States of America

ISBN: 0-87552-326-9

THE AUTHOR

Dr. Gordon R. Lewis, Professor of Theology at Conservative Baptist Theological Seminary in Denver, Colorado, hails from Johnson City, New York. He began his theological education there at Baptist Bible Seminary, earned the A.B. in Theology at Gordon College (1948) and the graduate B.Th. at Faith Theological Seminary (1951). Adding an A.M. in philosophy from Syracuse University (1953), he did work at Cornell University and culminated his philosophical studies with a Ph.D. from Syracuse (1959).

Before coming to the Denver Seminary in 1958, Dr. Lewis pastored the People's Baptist Church, Hamilton Park, Delaware (1949-51), and taught seven years at Baptist Bible Seminary as Professor of Apologetics and Philosophy. While teaching he has held several interim pastorates in New York and Colorado. His wife graduated from Shelton College where she majored in Christian Education. The family includes two girls and a boy.

Published articles by Professor Lewis have appeared in *The Collegiate Challenge, Christianity Today,* and the *Bulletin of the Evangelical Theological Society.* For his Master's thesis, he critically examined Reinhold Niebuhr's influential view of dialectical truth, and for his dissertation Augustine's classical position on faith and reason.

Elected to the Theta Beta Phi Honorary Philosophical Society of Syracuse University, Dr. Lewis is also a member of the American Philosophical Association, The Metaphysical Society of America, The American Academy of Religion, and the Evangelical Theological Society.

PREFACE

Of little value are religious discussions which misrepresent positions, magnify incidentals, or manifest poor spirit. This study attempts to avoid all three pitfalls. A fair hearing is given to the group's primary sources. To eliminate unimportant issues attention has been focused upon the Bible's unique authority and the gospel's central claims. The intention has been to set forth the gospel to others in the same spirit the author would like to meet in those who differ with him.

Beliefs on which a person stakes his spiritual life for time and eternity necessarily concern him deeply. Because these issues are so important, it is hoped that each reader — whatever his emotional involvements — will carefully consider the scriptural conditions of eternal life.

Use of the term "cult" is not intended to disparage any person or association of persons. It is meant to point up a difference not covered by "denomination." Christian denominations, in spite of their intramural debates on other theological and ecclesiastical matters, give preeminence to the gospel of Christ. Cults, on the other hand, while claiming to be Christian alter or minimize the core of Christian faith — the gospel. This study goes forth with the prayer that all who claim to be followers of Christ may personally trust the Savior who was God, became flesh, died for our sins, and rose again, according to the Scriptures.

The author wishes to express his gratitude to the Reverend Edward L. Hayes, Associate Professor of Christian Education at Conservative Baptist Theological Seminary, for preparing the sections entitled "Teaching Suggestions."

The Biblical citations, unless otherwise indicated, are from the King James Version.

Part V

The Bible, The Christian, and
Seventh-day Adventists
or
Is Seventh-day Adventism Evangelical?

In a sound Baptist church just prior to the Sunday morning service a mature deacon loudly acclaimed the message he had just heard on a radio broadcast called "The Voice of Prophecy." Upon learning that it was Seventh-day Adventist he was chagrined. Unsuspecting evangelicals may be equally impressed with the Adventists' television program, "Faith for Today," or personal copies of the Review and Herald Publishing Association's *Bible Readings for the Home Circle.*

Evangelicals also may be counted among the avid readers of some of the Adventists' strikingly beautiful magazines: *Life and Health,* a national journal, *Signs of the Times,* a prophetic monthly, *These Times,* dedicated to strengthening the moral, physical and spiritual life of the individual reader, and *Liberty,* a magazine of religious freedom.

All these sources have much truth in them. They have far more truth than the propaganda of other cults. As a matter of fact, they have so much truth that Christian laymen may be excused for asking if Adventists are not, after all, evangelical. And laymen have the company of some ministerial leaders in challenging the customary designation of Seventh-day Adventism as a cult.

In order to determine the facts of the matter Rev. Walter R. Martin and the late Donald Grey Barnhouse for two years probed Adventism's leading spokesmen. In September, 1956, an editorial in *Eternity* magazine stated Dr. Barnhouse's tradition-breaking conclusion. No longer can Seventh-day Adventists be classed as a cult and its adherents non-Christian, he declared. Adventists are "redeemed brethren and members of the body of Christ."[1] And Walter Martin, who had roundly denounced Christian Science and Jehovah's Witnesses as cults, now argued as vehemently that Seventh-day Adventism is evangelical. In spite of some secondary deviations from orthodox Christian teaching, Martin said, the Adventists "have always as a majority, held to the cardinal, fundamental doctrines of the Christian faith which are necessary to salvation, and to growth in grace that characterizes all true Christian believers."[2]

The Adventists' response to Martin appeared in a 700-page volume called *Questions on Doctrine*. "Prepared by a Representative Group of Seventh-day Adventist Leaders, Bible Teachers and Editors," the book came out in 1957 from the Washington, D. C., Review and Herald Publishing Association. Although not an official statement adopted by the General Conference in quadrennial session, "this volume can be viewed as truly representative of the faith and beliefs of the Seventh-day Adventist Church."[3]

Three years and much controversy later, Zondervan Publishing House printed Martin's complete analysis, *The Truth About Seventh-day Adventism*. The "Foreword" by Dr. Barnhouse narrowed the previous thesis that the majority of Adventists had always held an evangelical position. He wrote, "Let it be understood that we made only one claim; i.e., that those Seventh-day Adventists who follow the Lord in the same way as their leaders who have interpreted for us the doctrinal position of their church, are to be considered true members of the body of Christ."[4] In supporting this thesis Martin explicitly assumes: (1) that the Adventist leaders contacted were honest and (2) that *Questions on Doctrine* is "*the* primary source upon which to ground an evaluation of Adventist theology."[5] On this basis Martin concluded the leadership is evangelical, and as we shall see, evangelical with an Arminian system of theology which denies eternal security.

But not all evangelicals were willing to grant these assumptions or, if they did, not all concurred in Martin's conclusion. That conclusion was challenged by Professor Harold Lindsell, then Dean of Fuller Theological Seminary, in *Christianity Today*, March 31, 1958. Dr. Lindsell concurred that Seventh-day Adventism is not a cult like Christian Science or Jehovah's Witnesses, since it does not deny the absolute deity of Christ nor reject His atoning sacrifice on Calvary. But, Lindsell suggested, Seventh-day Adventism is not therefore evangelical. Like Romanism, it denies the sufficiency of Christ's death for man's salvation. Mixing works with grace Adventism errs with the legalism Paul disputed in Galatians. Grace simply supports man's will so that through his good works he may obtain eternal life. Works remain the basis of man's hope.[6] This differs from Arminianism, which makes faith as distinct from works the single condition of salvation.

Herbert S. Bird, home from a decade of missionary service, acknowledged that evangelicals have much to learn from Seventh-day Adventism, but concluded, an approach "which views it as just another evangelical denomination cannot help but bring about greater confusion in the Christian world than exists already."[7] The reasons for this judgment are given more fully in Bird's book entitled, *Theology of Seventh-day Adventism*, published by Eerdmans in 1961. The strongest of these is Adventism's legalism,

> Here not even the ninety-nine percent is necessarily a passing grade. In all probability the Galatian Judaizers, whose message the apostle Paul anathematized, agreed with him on almost everything but the one issue of the necessity of circumcision and the observance of sundry ceremonial practices for salvation. Wherefore, then, Paul's refusal to admit their teaching is essentially Christian and to move themselves into the group of those who are brethren in Christ? . . . The reason is that for Paul the problem was not that of the number of doctrines on which the people agreed with Biblical Christianity, but that of whether the details on which they disagreed, whether these details were few or many, were in areas of truth so vital that their denial subverted the gospel of the grace of God.[8]

In reviewing Martin's book, *The Truth About Seventh-day Adventism*, Dr. Merrill Tenney, Professor of New Testament at Wheaton College, raised a question about Martin's second assumption. "Is the doctrinal platform of Seventh-day Adventism determined by what a few of its scholars defined, or by what the majority of its followers believe and practice?" Tenney apparently feels that though Martin did not compromise on the level of the leaders' teaching, he failed to give sufficient consideration to the movement's policies and practices and to the bulk of its teachings.[9]

Norman F. Douty, in a book entitled *Another Look at Seventh-day Adventism* (Baker Book House, 1962), not limiting himself to *Questions on Doctrine,* found that the movement denied doctrines the church has always declared, and taught doctrines the church as a whole has always denied. In spite of the differences he said, "It is our duty to manifest love and kindness toward those who are in Adventism."[10] But Douty concluded, "They who would be loyal to God rather than be swayed by sentiment must avoid any alliance with the Adventist system. No other course is open to them."[11]

And in 1963 Anthony A. Hoekma, Associate Professor of Systematic Theology at Calvin Theological Seminary, published a book categorizing Seventh-day Adventism as one of *The Four Major Cults.* Any group in which five specified criteria play a leading role he classifies as a cult. On each count Hoekema finds Seventh-day Adventism guilty, although with inconsistency and ambivalence. The five tests: An extra-biblical source of authority, denial of justification by grace alone, devaluation of Christ, the group as the exclusive community of the saved, and the group's central role in eschatology.[12] Because Hoekema's conclusions are carefully stated and reveal some of the specific problems to look for in studying Adventism, they deserve our careful attention.

Seventh-day Adventists do have an extra-Scriptural source of authority in the writings of Ellen G. White, which are accepted by them as inspired counsels from the Lord.[13]

Though Seventh-day Adventists claim to teach justification by grace alone their doctrine of the investigative judgment and their views of the sabbath command are inconsistent with that claim.[14]

While appreciating the Adventist's recognition of Christ as fully divine, however, we must reluctantly observe that there are aspects of Seventh-day Adventist teaching which detract from the splendor of Christ's deity and do in fact constitute a devaluation of Him.[15]

Though theoretically granting that people outside their community can be saved Seventh-day Adventists actually undermine that concession by their teaching on the remnant church. Since they claim to be *the* remnant church in distinction from all other Christian bodies, they do manifest the cultist trait under discussion, though in a somewhat ambivalent manner.[16]

For Seventh-day Adventists . . . eschatology is the arena in which the glorification of their own movement completes itself and in which they shall be completely vindicated over against their enemies. Since the Sabbath will be the great test of loyalty in the last days, we see that the antithesis between God and Satan becomes in the end the antithesis between Seventh-day Adventism and those who refuse to follow its special teaching. We conclude that since Seventh-day Adventists do picture themselves as playing a central role in eschatology this distinctive trait of the cult is also clearly applicable to their movement.[17]

This brief sketch of the revolutionary attempt to regard Seventh-day Adventism evangelical and of its disclaimers reveals some of the issues which must now be faced in any study of that movement. Our answer to these issues will determine our approach to Adventist friends. If they are still considered non-Christian cultists we shall endeavor to win them to the Lord. If they are classed with Romanists in their legalism we must approach them as Paul did the people at Galatia. If they are evangelical we may fellowship and work together in the evangelistic cause while engaging in intramural debates on issues not affecting salvation. Or it may be that no generalization can be made about the movement as a whole, and we must deal with each individual upon the basis of his own stated beliefs.

The approach of *Confronting the Cults* suggests seven questions to use in discussion with people to help distinguish cultic from Christian organizations and lead people to Christ. Evangelicals may use these questions to guide discussions they may have with Adventists.

Authority

What must a man do to be saved? Our answer to that question is determined by its source and basis. To help Adventists see where their controversial beliefs may have arisen we must ask, "Do you base your teachings on revelations or sacred writings other than the Bible?"

In answer, Adventists usually present one of their "Fundamental Beliefs." The group's official denominational teaching states "that the Holy Scriptures of the Old and New Testaments were given of God, contain an all-sufficient revelation of His will to men, and are the only unerring rule of faith and practice (II Tim. 3: 15-16)."[18] Among the doctrines shared with conservative Christians, the writer of *Questions on Doctrine* included this, "That the Scriptures are the inspired revelation of God to men; and that the Bible is the sole rule of faith and practice."[19] To be even more explicit they add, "We belive that all theological beliefs must be measured by the living Word, judged by its truth, and whatsoever is unable to pass this test, or is found to be out of harmony with its message is to be rejected."[20]

Despite these strong affirmations of the supremacy and sufficiency of Scripture, ambiguity persists concerning the status of Ellen G. White's writings. Because Adventists believe Mrs. White had the gift of prophecy (Eph. 4:11), she is called a prophetess. She gave "testimonies" as did the prophets throughout the Old Testament (Rev. 10:10),[21] and entitled one of her works, *Testimonies*. In a popular booklet, *Your Friends the Adventists*, Arthur S. Maxwell remarks about the "authority" of Mrs. White's works and adds, "Many believe that Mrs. White spoke with more than human wisdom. Read one of her books yourself and see what you think."[22] The writers of *Questions on Doctrine* hold her writings in "highest esteem" because "the Holy Spirit opened to her mind important events and called her to give certain instructions for these last days." Consequently, "we as a denomination accept them as inspired counsels from the Lord. But we have never equated them with Scripture."[23]

If Mrs. White's writings are not equivalent to Scripture why are both said to be "inspired"? Walter R. Martin sympathetically reasons that "inspiration" in connection with Mrs. White's works "has a rather different meaning from the inspiration of the Bible." Nevertheless, even Martin concludes that "the Adventists are defending a situation which is at best paradoxical and at times contradictory."[24] Until this confusion is cleared up in their statements about inspiration it is difficult to understand without qualification the Adventist's claim "that we do not regard the writings of Ellen G. White as an addition to the sacred canon of Scripture . . . in the same sense as the Holy Scriptures."[25]

In order to help Seventh-day Adventists more clearly to distinguish Mrs. White from the Biblical prophets and thus avoid cultism we may ask a question suggested by Dr. Harold Lindsell. "Did Mrs. White err at any point theologically or in ethical and personal life, or was she inerrant in all her teachings, pronouncements and ethics?"[26] If Adventists continue to defend her every word and action they put her on a pedestal even higher than the Christian Scientists put Mary Baker Eddy or the Latter-day Saints put Joseph Smith. To regard Mrs. White, or any such person, as God's single spokesman for the end times is to supplant the ultimate authority of Scripture. If one differs with Mrs. White does he necessarily differ with God?

The evidence does not support Mrs. White's infallibility. Adventists cannot simply assume "that Mrs. White's writings are free from theological and exegetical errors," Walter Martin points out, "*for they are not.*"[27] This charge is documented, for one thing, by indications of plagiarism. In parallel columns Martin lists passages from Mrs. White and from Conybeare and Howson's *The Life and Epistles of the Apostle Paul*, J. A. Wylie's *History of the Waldenses*, and D'Aubigne's *History of the Reformation*.[28] Then, on Mrs. White's own authority it may be shown that she erred, even in her "inspired" *Testimonies*. She admitted, "Under these circumstances I yielded my judgment to that of others and wrote what appeared in Number Eleven in regard to the Health Institute, being unable to give all that I had seen. *In this I did wrong.*"[29] Who can say that Mrs. White did not yield upon other occasions to the pressure of circumstances or opinions in exercising her "gift of prophecy"?

May God help any Adventists who have not already done so to admit as plainly as did Mrs. White her fallibility. Then they cannot establish doctrine on her authority, but must always discover doctrine in Scripture and test her works by Scripture. Any Adventist who confesses this and dispenses with the proof texts from Mrs. White shows that he holds the Bible alone infallible and sufficient to all matters of faith and practice. As far as this point is concerned, such Adventists are welcome to the camp of evangelicals. But any Adventist who continues to equivocate on the inerrancy of Mrs. White thereby excludes himself from unqualified acceptance among evangelicals. Our prayer is that every Adventist would in fact hold that there is but *one* infallible rule of faith and practice, the Bible, and so on this issue be evangelical.

11

The Gospel's Priority

Another question must be asked Adventists, "Is your primary business preaching the gospel?"

Many evangelicals would expect a sincere Adventist answer to say their main business was preaching the law. Some have wondered whether the Adventists' radio and television ministry was truly representative of their beliefs. The Adventist leaders faced this forthright question:

> Are not the spiritual content and evangelical emphasis of your "Voice of Prophecy" radio program and "Faith for Today" telecast a rather far cry from the doctrinal and legal core of Adventism? Are they not rather a bid for good will, and subtle attempt to draw those who enroll in your proffered Bible courses to gradually accept the doctrinal and legal heart of Adventism?

To this frank question, the Adventists replied:

> There is no attempt at subtlety or effort to deceive. The heart of the Advent message is Christ and Him crucified . . . We believe that Christianity is a real experience with Christ. Christianity is a relationship to a Person — our blessed Lord and Saviour Jesus Christ . . . We also believe that a specific message is due the world today, and that we were called into being to have a part in proclaiming it. But again, that that message is simply the everlasting gospel in the setting of God's great judgment hour, the imminent second coming of our Lord, and the preparation of men to meet God . . . We repeat, this emphasis is not something subtle, as suggested in the question. It is not a lure, or trick, or bait. It is, instead, a serious endeavor to put first things definitely first in our public presentations, and to let the world see and know that the heart burden of Adventism is Christ and His salvation.[30]

Plainly, the writers of *Questions on Doctrine* intend that the primary business of the Adventists is preaching not law, but gospel.

The same conclusion is required by Arthur S. Maxwell's essay entitled, "What is a Seventh-day Adventist?" In a series on different religions in a popular magazine, Maxwell wrote:

> A Seventh-day Adventist is one who, having accepted Christ as his personal Savior, walks in humble obedience to the will of God as revealed in the Holy Scriptures. A Bible-loving Christian, he seeks to pattern his life according to the teachings of this book, while looking

for the imminent return of his Lord. He lives under a sense of destiny, believing it is his duty to warn mankind that the end of the world is at hand.[31]

Unless one presumes adversely to judge the motivation of these leaders, he can conclude that as they see it, their primary business is preaching the gospel. If keeping the seventh day or an Old Testament diet appears to be the prominent feature, we may have misjudged. Or there may be differences in the movement itself. On the leaders' own affirmation of the priority of the gospel, we must conclude that those they represent do take an evangelical stance. It may be wise to reserve final judgment, however, until we have analyzed more fully their position on the elements of the gospel message.

Christ

One basic element of the gospel which in the New Testament distinguished true Christianity from counterfeits concerned the nature of Jesus Christ. Let us ask Adventists, then, this leading question: "Do you believe that Jesus is the Messiah, the Christ, the eternal Word who has come in the flesh?" What answer may be anticipated?

Among the Adventist's "Fundamental Beliefs" is this fine summary of Biblical teaching:

> Jesus Christ is very God, being of the same nature and essence as the Eternal Father. While retaining His divine nature He took upon Himself the nature of the human family, lived on the earth as a man, exemplified in His life as our example the principles of righteousness, attested His relationship to God by many mighty miracles, died for our sins on the cross, was raised from the dead, and ascended to the Father, where He ever lives to make intercession for us.[32]

On the deity of Christ and the fact of His incarnation Seventh-day Adventists stand squarely with evangelical Christians. The Biblical doctrines are made explicit objects of faith for salvation in Scripture, the Adventists assert. By the Scriptural test adopted in this study, then, Adventists in their view of Christ's Person are evangelical.

Some critics of Adventism, however, in evaluating the movement employ the more detailed and full doctrinal statements. By these standards the Adventists' understanding of Christ's human nature is challenged. The Adventists differ from the historic Christian church in their notion of human nature, and consequently in their doctrine of Christ's human nature. Man is not an entity with two parts, a body and a soul. They teach that "the soul of man represents the whole man, and not a particular part independent of the other component parts of man's nature; and further that the soul cannot exist apart from the body, for man is a unity."[33] When Christ became man, He took upon Him human flesh and human nature, but no human soul as a distinct immaterial substance. In the final judgment of Norman F. Douty, then, the Adventist's doctrine is like that of Apollinaris, whose view was pronounced heretical by the church.[34] To the early Christians this teaching detracted from Christ's full humanity. The orthodox doctrine maintains that Christ took upon Himself not only a human body, but also a human soul or spirit.

A second aspect of Adventist teaching about Christ has been criticized. While orthodox Christians have held that His human nature was like that of Adam before the fall, Adventists have held it was like that of Adam and the race after the fall. It was necessary for Christ to share fallen human nature, Adventists insist, in order to be tempted in all points as we are. Numerous quotations in standard Adventists' writings are cited by Bird and Douty to the effect that Christ had a sinful nature.[35]

Of course the Bible teaches Christ had no sin. The child born of Mary was not sinful but holy (Lk. 1:35). Jesus said Satan had nothing in Him (Jn. 14:30). Peter called Him a lamb "without blemish and without spot" (I Pet. 1:19) and declared He did no sin, "neither was guile found in his mouth" (I Pet 2:22). And John who knew him so well could write, "In him is no sin" (I Jn. 3:5).

Seventh-day Adventist writers unite in affirming that Christ never sinned, but they may contradict each other on the issue of the sinfulness of his human nature. The writers of *Questions on Doctrine*, however, adopt the orthodox position and insist that Christ took sinless human nature.[36] In alluding to Christ's sinful human nature other Adventists denied the least participation in

14

sin, but assumed Christ suffered the liabilities inherent in human nature. Christ was genuinely tempted in all points as men are tempted, and identified Himself with the sinners He came to save.[37]

In their views of Christ, then, are Adventists evangelical? If to be evangelical one must affirm the full details of orthodox doctrine, then on one point they fall short. They do not assert that Christ took a human spirit or soul as an immaterial substance distinct from the human body in His incarnation. The leaders who wrote *Questions on Doctrine* emphatically deny that His nature was sinful. For those they represent, the one issue that remains can hardly of itself exclude from evangelicalism people who affirm the absolute deity of Christ, the doctrine of the Trinity and the literal incarnation.

Historically, there have been sound men who have held a similar view of the soul, and some hold it today. Biblically, Adventists receive the Word who was God and became flesh (Jn. 1:1, 12,14). Who then, when thinking of their view of Christ, can say that they have not the authority to be called sons of God? They affirm that Jesus has come in the flesh (I Jn. 4:1-3). Who then will say that they are antichrist? They believe that Jesus is the Christ (Jn. 20:31). Who then will dare to question whether they have life through His name? On this issue it appears that Bird and Douty either raise too detailed a standard for evangelicalism, or have abandoned the issue concerning the Adventist's evangelicalism. If the Adventists represented by *Questions on Doctrine* are not part of the body of Christ, it is not because of their view of Christ's Person. Christians will not initially help Adventists by debating these detailed issues about Christ's human nature. Rather, Christians should rejoice in the testimony of an Adventist's belief in Christ's deity and incarnation, and move on to other issues.

Redemption

The gospel includes an affirmation not only concerning Christ's person, but also concerning His work. Christians interested in helping Adventists will ask: Do you believe Christ's shed blood is the only basis for the forgiveness of your sins?

A similar question came to the leaders: "Seventh-day Adventists have frequently been charged with teaching that the atonement was not completed on the cross. Is this charge true?"[37] The answer was as blunt. "May we state most earnestly and explicitly that Seventh-day Adventists do *not* believe that Christ made but a partial or incomplete sacrificial atonement on the cross."[38] What they do stress, is the difference between Christ's completed work and its application to individuals.

> Most decidedly the all-sufficient atoning sacrifice of Jesus our Lord was *offered and completed* on the cross of Calvary. This was done for all mankind. (Jn. 2:2). But this sacrificial work will actually benefit human hearts *only* as we surrender our lives to God and experience the miracle of the new birth. In this experience Jesus our High Priest *applies to us the benefits* of His atoning sacrifice. Our sins are forgiven, we become children of God by faith in Christ Jesus, and the peace of God dwells in our hearts.[39]

Clearly this is an evangelical position as stated. If, however, the application of the atonement's saving benefits depends upon some additional work of Christ, such as the alleged cleansing of the heavenly sanctuary in 1944, it raises the issue of the completeness of the work at Calvary. Furthermore, if eventually all sin must be put upon Satan as a scapegoat, the atonement at the cross seems incomplete.

How did the ideas of the investigative judgment in the heavenly sanctuary and the scapegoat originate? Adventists interpreted the Old Testament day of atonement typologically. On that day participants were judged (Lev. 23:29-30) and the goat was sent off into the wilderness (Lev. 16:20-28). Typological interpretations of these events (rather than explicit Scriptural teaching) became the basis of doctrine.[40] How this developed is a story in itself.

In 1844, because of William Miller's prediction of the end of the world, a flurry of excitement ended in a great disappointment. Miller had found a basis for predicting Christ's return in Daniel 8:14. The 2300 days until the cleansing of the sanctuary were taken to be 2300 years. Starting at 457 B.C., when Artaxerxes decreed the Israelites could rebuild their ruined capital city, the period ended in 1844. But Jesus did not return to Jerusalem.

On October 23, 1844, the day following the scheduled return of Christ, a Millerite named Hiram Edson walked alone through a cornfield, when,

16

suddenly there burst upon his mind the thought that there were *two* phases to Christ's ministry in the heaven of heavens, just as in the earthly sanctuary of old . . . He (Christ) for the first time *entered* on that day the second apartment of that (heavenly) sanctuary to perform in the Most Holy before coming to this earth.[41]

But what in the heavenly sanctuary needed to be cleansed? Explaining this, Mrs. White wrote, "Sin was not canceled by the blood of the victim. A means was thus provided by which *it was transferred to the sanctuary.* By the offering of blood, the sinner was not yet entirely released from the condemnation of the law."[42] Since the record of good and evil deeds still stands in heaven, the authors of *Questions on Doctrine* admit, "Acceptance of Christ at conversion does not seal a person's destiny."[43]

Pardon from all sin as a benefit of Christ's atonement, according to Adventists, is not received upon believing. Justification before God Himself in the holy of holies awaits another work of Christ, His investigative judgment. There even the believer may lose his salvation. "When any have sins remaining upon the books of record, unrepented of and unforgiven, their names will be blotted out of the book of life, and the record of their good deeds will be erased from the book of God's remembrance."[44]

On what basis do men stand or fall in the investigative judgment? Not their union with Christ by faith, not their new birth by the Holy Spirit, not their propitiation by the blood of Christ, say Seventh-day Adventists. "The law of God is the standard by which the characters and the lives of men will be tested in the judgment."[45] Ameliorating this, Adventists emphasize that Christ the great high priest becomes the believer's advocate, and in the heavenly court He never lost a case. But this comfort is snatched away when they add, "To us, it seems clear that we must continue our allegiance throughout life if we expect Christ to represent us in the judgment."[46] Quite the contrary, the Bible explains that it is precisely because no sinner could keep the law that we need an advocate in case he sins. "My little children, these things I write unto you that ye sin not, And if any man sin, we have an advocate with the Father, Jesus Christ the righteous" (I Jn. 2:1).

So long as the outcome of the investigative judgment is determined not by faith, but by law-keeping, it is difficult to conclude that Adventists consistently regard the blood of Christ the sole ground for salvation. Evangelicals must confront Adventists, not so much with their error in timing divine judgment or their literalistic concept of the heavenly sanctuary or the unwise practice of basing a major doctrine on an Old Testament type alone, but with their consequent contradiction of Scriptural teaching on justification by faith. That involves complete pardon from all sin and the imputation of Christ's perfect righteousness. So a believer in Christ, crucified and risen, need never fear judgment or condemnation (Rom. 8:1; Jn. 3:18). "Be it known unto you therefore, men and brethren, that through this man is preached unto you the forgiveness of sins: and by him all that believe are justified from all things from which ye could not be justified by the law of Moses." In the context of Acts 13:38-39 "law of Moses" is not distinct from, but includes the Ten Commandments. Let Adventists hear again Romans 3:38, "Therefore we conclude that a man is justified by faith without the deeds of the law." (Cf. Rom. 4:6; 11:6; Eph. 2:2-9; Gal. 2:16; Tit. 3:5.) Whatever Daniel 8:14 may mean, it cannot overthrow the foundational teaching throughout Scripture that the just shall live by faith in Christ's complete atoning work, not in their ability to keep the law. Believers have redemption "through his blood, the forgiveness of sins, according to the riches of his grace" (Eph. 1:7).

Where then does the scapegoat come in? The name of the goat the high priest sent out into the wilderness on the day of atonement was Azazel. Adventists, as well as many orthodox interpreters, think Azazel designates Satan.[47] The meaning of the name is not the crucial issue. Do Adventists hold that Satan in some way provides atonement for sin not completed by Christ?

Contemporary Adventists as represented by the authors of *Questions on Doctrine* flatly deny that Satan in any way completes the atonement. But, they say, Satan is not unrelated to our sin. In all sin, they teach, there is a twofold responsibility: "first my responsibility as the *perpetrator*, agent, or medium; and second, Satan's responsibility as the instigator, or temptor, in whose heart sin was first conceived."[48] So when Satan is said to carry away our sins, they mean he is paying for instigating them, not that he is providing an atonement for them. "Satan makes no atonement for our sins. But Satan will ultimately have to bear the retributive punishment for his responsibility in the sins of all men, both righteous and wicked."[49]

18

For two reasons, Adventists argue, Satan could not be a vicarious sin-bearer: (1) the transaction with the scapegoat took place *after* the atonement had been accomplished, and (2) it was not slain—and without the shedding of blood there is no remission (Heb. 9:22). Seventh-day Adventists therefore repudiate *in toto* any idea, suggestion, or implication that Satan is in any sense or degree our sin-bearer. The thought is abhorrent to us, and appallingly sacrilegious."[50] On this basis then, evangelical Christians may choose not to follow the Adventist's interpretation of the scapegoat, but they cannot justifiably charge those who accept it with heresy affecting salvation. One could only wish their position on the investigative judgment was as emphatically aligned with Biblical teaching on Christ's atonement. On that point the denomination has yet consistently to state the evangelical position. Its legalism is further considered in question seven.

The Resurrection of Christ

Faith in another aspect of the gospel, Christ's triumph over the grave, is an explicit condition of salvation (Rom. 10:9). Out of concern for an Adventist, then, ask, "Do you believe that Jesus Christ rose from the dead?"

In agreement with orthodox Christians, Adventists hold "that Jesus Christ arose literally and bodily from the grave."[51] To avoid possible misunderstanding they further explain, "The resurrection of Christ is not to be understood in a spiritual sense. He actually rose from the dead. He who came from the tomb was the *same* Jesus who lived here in the flesh."[52] In support of the resurrection Adventists amass the same evidences as evangelicals, and they take a similar position on its doctrinal significance. The strongest opponents of Adventism do not question the Adventist's belief in Christ's resurrection. So evangelicals will rejoice that their faith in Christ's victory over death is shared by Seventh-day Adventists.

Personal Trust

Christians concerned to win not mere arguments, but persons, may also ask Adventists, "Are you personally trusting Jesus Christ as your redeemer and Lord?"

Much like evangelicals, Adventists repeatedly stress the indispensability of faith.[53] In those discussions Hebrews 11:3 frequently occurs, "Without faith it is impossible to please God." Furthermore they distinguish between a mere intellectual belief and total commitment. Mrs. White explained that there is

> a kind of belief that is wholly distinct from faith. The existence and power of God, the truth of His Word, are facts that even Satan and his hosts cannot at heart deny. The Bible says that "the devils also believe and tremble"; but this is not faith. Where there is not only a belief in God's Word, but a submission of will to Him; where the heart is yielded to Him, the affections fixed upon Him, there is faith, — faith that works by love, and purifies the soul.[54]

A similar emphasis upon both belief and faith appears in Mrs. White's famous *Steps to Christ.*[55]

And in *Questions on Doctrine* justification is said to be by a faith that lays hold upon the power of God.

> Even in the days of old, men were not justified by works; they were justified by faith" (Heb. 2:4; compare Rom. 1:17; Gal. 3:8, 11; Phil. 3:9; Heb. 10:38). God calls upon man to be righteous; but man is naturally unrighteous. If he is to be prepared for the kingdom of God, he must be made righteous. This is something man cannot do in and of himself. He is unclean and unrighteous. The more he works, and the greater his effort, the more he reveals the unrighteousness of his own heart. Therefore, if man is ever to become righteous, it must be by a power entirely outside himself — it must be by the power of God.[56]

With the Seventh-day Adventist view of faith as such, evangelicals do not take issue. But evangelicals know that it is one thing to preach the need for personal faith and another to exercise that faith personally. In conversations with Adventists as with others we may help by testifying of our own unconditional trust in our living Lord.

Faith Alone

For Adventists the final question becomes crucial. "Do you depend upon some achievements of your own to contribute to salvation or is it only by God's grace through faith?"

Many Adventist statements related works to faith in an orthodox manner. In *Steps to Christ* Mrs. White wrote:

> There are two errors against which the children of God — particularly those who have just come to trust His grace —especially need to guard. The first, . . . is that of looking to their own works, trusting to anything they can do, to bring themselves into harmony with God. He who is trying to become holy by his own works in keeping the law, is attempting an impossibility. All that man can do without Christ is polluted by selfishness and sin. It is the grace of Christ alone, through faith, that can make us holy.
>
> The opposite and no less dangerous error is, that belief in Christ releases men from keeping the law of God; that since by faith alone we become partakers of the grace of Christ, our works have nothing to do with our redemption.
>
> But notice here that obedience is not a mere outward compliance, but the service of love. The law of God is an expression of His very nature . . . If our hearts are renewed in the likeness of God, . . . will not the law of God be carried out in life? . . . Obedience - the service and allegiance of love - is the true sign of discipleship . . . Instead of releasing man from obedience, it is faith, and faith only, that makes us partakers of the grace of Christ which enables us to render obedience.[57]

"The faith which justifies," comments *Bible Readings for the Home Circle* on Galations 5:6, "is the faith which works."[58] Arthur S. Maxwell explains, "Acceptance of divine grace brings a man under a thousandfold greater compulsion to obey God — the compulsion not of force but of love . . . Being under grace is not an excuse for sin, but an added reason for righteous living."[59] Asked point-blank if Adventists teach that people must obey the Ten Commandments in order to be saved, Maxwell answered,

> No. Salvation is by grace alone. There is only one way of salvation. That is faith in the atoning death of Jesus Christ. No one can "work his way" into the kingdom of God. No degree of obedience, no works of penance, no amount of money entitles anyone to any divine favor. Nevertheless, "faith without works is dead." Keeping the commandments is the result, the evidence, of salvation. It is a matter of love, not legal duty. "If ye love me," said Jesus, "keep my commandments" (Jn. 14:15).[60]

21

And the contributors to *Questions on Doctrine* concur:

> Salvation is not now, and has never been, by law or works; salvation is only by the grace of Christ . . . Nothing men can do, or have done, can in any way *merit* salvation. While works are not a *means* of salvation, good works are the inevitable *result* of salvation. However, these good works are possible only for the child of God whose life is inwrought by the Spirit of God . . . This relationship and sequence is imperative, but is often misunderstood or reversed.[61]

Even as the fruit of faith, however, Adventists do not expect believers to keep all the varied commands of the Old Testament. The ceremonial law of Moses as distinct from the moral law of God in the Ten Commandments, was but a shadow of Christ's work to come. Since His crucifixion the ceremonial law has been done away. It is carnal and enslaves anyone who attempts to keep it. But the Ten Commandments are not abolished. They are spiritual and bless with liberty the one who keeps them."[62] With a different interpretation of the fourth commandment many orthodox Christians would agree with this distinction. Others would insist that even the Old Testament moral law as stated in the Ten Commandments inscribed in stone is done away (II Cor. 3), but nine of the Ten Commandments are then maintained as stated in the New Testament.

But one wonders how the Adventists, consistent with their own view, advocate Old Testament dietary requirements. Some Adventists may declare their freedom from them as legal taboos, but find the distinction between clean and unclean animals prior to Moses and keep them as a health program.[63] But a popular booklet sent by the Adventists to a letter of inquiry teaches something quite different. In *Just What Do You Believe About Your Church?* Fordyce W. Detamore writes:

> As long as Isaiah 66:15-17 is in this Book, how dare I tell you it doesn't make any difference whether or not you eat swine's flesh and other unclean foods? . . . It would be much easier for me to say, "Go ahead and eat as you please; you needn't worry about those things any more." But God says those who are eating unclean things when He comes will be destroyed. Wouldn't you rather I put it plainly so that you'll not be deceived and be destroyed at our Lord's coming?[64]

Threats like this are difficult to harmonize with the assurances that salvation is by grace through faith and not of works.

The same confusion seems to exist with respect to the Ten Commandments. On one page Detamore says, "We keep the law of God because we are saved, not because we can save ourselves by lawkeeping." But on another page he asserts, "Everywhere the Bible stresses the imperativeness of obedience if one would be saved." He concludes a section captioned "Standard of Judgment":

> The best summary of the requirements for salvation is found in the counsel Jesus gave the rich young nobleman (Matthew 19:15-21), "If thou wilt enter into life, (1) keep the commandments, . . . and (2) follow me." There is no other hope of salvation. By the standard of God's holy law we shall be judged in the day of reckoning.[65]

In order to help, observe that no human has ever kept the law. No one was ever saved by keeping its requirements. It actually serves not to save but to show men how desperately they need to be saved. The law speaks "that all the world may become guilty before God. Therefore by the deeds of the law shall no flesh be justified in his sight: for by the law is the knowledge of sin" (Rom. 3:19-20). By quoting the commandments Christ sought to show the rich young ruler his need of "righteousness without the law . . . even the righteousness of God which is by faith of Jesus Christ unto all and upon all them that believe" (Rom. 3:20-21). The young man's claim to have kept all the law from his youth revealed his failure to perceive its fundamental import. This Jesus brought out by asking him to sell all that he possessed, and give it to the poor. Sorrowfully he did not love God with his whole heart or his neighbor as himself. But upon these two commandments rests the whole law (Mt. 22:37-40).

The acid test of Adventist views on the law is the doctrine of the Sabbath. From the creation to the end times the fourth commandment is held to be part of God's unchanging moral law. Roman Catholic papal authority changed the day of worship from Saturday to Sunday, Adventists teach. And Protestantism has not completed the reformation by continuing seventh-day worship. In the end times, now upon us, the truth is being restored. Those who receive this light and conviction are responsible for obedience to this command. As the final great religious crisis breaks upon mankind papal power will head up forces in opposition to God, requiring first-day worship (Dan. 7:25; Rev. 13:16,17) as the mark of the beast. At this future time the day of worship will be a worldwide test of loyalty to Christ or antichrist.[66]

Those who do not now see the obligation of the fourth commandment are not punished, but in the future crisis Sunday worship will be sufficient grounds for condemnation. Then all who keep the commandments of God (Rev. 12:17) will join the remnant church in worshiping on Saturday. Unquestionably salvation in the future is by faith and Saturday worship, by grace and law keeping. While at present God overlooks Sunday worshipers' ignorance, and does not execute the deserved penalty for flaunting His commandment, the Sunday worshipers have in fact committed gross sin. All evangelicals are still daughters of Babylon; they bear the mark of the beast. This, Herbert S. Bird predicts, "will not appeal to many as being a solid basis for Christian fellowship."[67] And it is not more solid for asserting without qualification that salvation is by grace through faith.

The Adventist's case for seventh-day worship does not hold up. If the fourth commandment is a moral principle it may be kept by worship on one day of the seven, Sunday. Nowhere does the New Testament reaffirm the fourth commandment, although it repeats the other nine. As a matter of fact whoever makes sabbath days a test of fellowship disobeys the New Testament. And in the Biblical context weekly sabbaths are not excluded (Col. 2:13-17; Gal. 4:9-11; Rom. 13:8-10; 14:4-6,10,12,13).

Considering the centuries of tradition in which the Jewish writers of the New Testament were saturated, it is remarkable that they so emphasized the first day of the week. On the first day Jesus rose from the dead (Jn. 20:1). He appeared to the ten disciples on that same day (Jn. 20:19). One week later he appeared to the eleven disciples (Jn. 20:26). The promised Pentecostal coming of the Holy Spirit occurred on Sunday (Lev. 23:16). That significant Sunday after the first message proclaiming Christ's death and resurrection, 3000 received the Word, were baptized and added to the church (Acts 2). At Troas the Christians assembled for worship the first day of the week (Acts 20:6-7). And on the first day of the week the Corinthians made their contributions. As the Sabbath commemorated not only creation but also divine deliverance from Egypt (Deut. 5:15) it is fitting that the first day commemorate the Creator's mighty deliverance of Christ from the grave.

24

The change in the day of worship was not made, as Adventists claim, centuries after New Testament times by the Pope. It was already in the New Testament and it was recognized by writers shortly thereafter. References to first-day worship may be found in the writings of Ignatius, Bishop of Antioch A.D. 110; Justin Martyr, A.D. 100-165; Barnabas, A.D. 120-150; Irenaeus, A.D. 178; Bardaisan, A.D. 154; Tertullian, A.D. 200; Origen, A.D. 225; Cyprian, A.D. 200-258; Peter of Alexandria, A.D. 300; and Eusebius, A.D. 315.[68]

These historical facts undermine the whole Adventist interpretation of first-day worship as the mark of the Beast. If the Roman Pope is the Beast, no particular significance can be attributed to his alleged change of the day of worship. And first-day worship cannot be any particular "mark" of the Beast. It follows that no special place can be given to the keeping of the fourth commandment in interpreting the reference to those who keep the commandments of God (Rev. 14:12). Neither is it necessary to apply the power designated in Daniel 7:25 to Rome.

The great test of allegiance to God distinctively proclaimed by Adventists is not an explicit, unmistakable Scriptural test. It is a theory of well-meaning, but mistaken men and women. No such human fabrication should be made a fundamental of faith, rending the body of Christ. And surely no such theory should be added to the simple gospel invitation. Salvation never has been or will be conditioned upon the seventh-day worship. Nowhere do we read, "Believe on the Lord Jesus Christ and keep the seventh day and thou shalt never come into condemnation." But repeatedly we read, "If there had been a law given which could have given life, verily righteousness should have been by the law. But the scripture hath concluded all under sin, that the promise by faith of Jesus might be given to them that believe (Gal. 3:21-22). However commendable a law may be, added to faith it destroy's God's way of salvation. The Bible teaches, "If by grace, then it is no more of works: otherwise grace is no more grace. But if it be of works, then is it no more grace: otherwise work is no more work" (Rom. 11:6). Much as we should like to say Adventists base their hope on grace alone, some of their positions on Old Testament dietary requirements and seventh-day worship seem to contradict it. Would to God that every Adventist could give the testimony of Rev. Don Phillips, who came to realize the full meaning of grace. In a *Power* account of his conversion from Seventh-day Adventism he testified, "It is wonderful to be free from legalism, and to *know* that I can serve and glorify Him (the Lord)."[69]

In view of apparent Adventist inconsistency on keeping the law for salvation, how can Walter R. Martin pronounce Adventism evangelical? Martin's judgment follows from his interpretation of the position in terms of Arminianism. Among evangelicals is a school of thought named after James Arminius (1560-1609) which opposes Calvinism's stress on divine election and eternal security. Arminians often deny eternal security, teaching that a person may believe, enjoy the saved life for a time, and then forfeit salvation by unbelief. Seventh-day Adventists classify themselves as Arminians. In *Questions on Doctrine* they teach,

> that God, by an eternal and unchangeable decree in Christ before the world was, determined to elect from the fallen and sinning human race to everlasting life those who through his grace believe in Jesus Christ and *persevere* in faith and obedience; and, on the contrary, had resolved to reject the unconverted and unbelievers.[70]

This seems to make divine election conditional not only upon faith, but continued works. In the judgment of Walter Martin, the Adventist position,

> though tinged with legalism has its roots in the basic Arminian position that one receives salvation as a free gift of God, but once he has received this gift, the believer is responsible for its maintenance and duration, and the chief means of accomplishing this is "commandment-keeping" or "obedience to all the laws of God."[71]

From this interpretation Martin's conclusion follows.

> Since Adventists are basically Arminian, we may logically deduce that, in a sense, their salvation rests upon legal grounds. But the saving factor in the dilemma is that by life and by world-wide witness, Adventists, like other so-called Arminians, give true evidence that they have experienced the "new birth" which is by grace alone, through faith in our Lord and His sacrifice upon the cross. One would be callous and uncharitable indeed not to accept their profession of dependence upon Christ alone for redemption, even though there *is inconsistency in their theological system.*[72]

While declaring Adventists evangelical, as sympathetic an interpreter as Martin admits their system is tinged with legalism and is contradictory. But over against this deficiency he sets their life and service. Others like Bird, Douty and Hoekema respect the life and service but feel the doctrinal divergence is far more serious than that between Calvinism and Arminianism. In pointing out Adventist errors, however, these writers do not regard *Questions on Doctrine* representative of Adventism or fail to limit marks of evangelism to Scripturally explicit conditions of eternal life.

In contrast, this study has evaluated the Seventh-day Adventism that is represented by *Questions on Doctrine* and has employed Scripturally explicit tests related to salvation for determining whether the movement is evangelical. What, then, are the results by these standards?

The Seventh-day Adventist position is evangelical in respect to statements about the priority of the gospel, the deity of the incarnate Christ, His substitutionary atonement, His resurrection from the dead and the necessity of personal faith in Christ.

One can hardly acknowledge the many agreements with evangelical and orthodox theology and at the same time class the Adventists with cults which deny the priority of the gospel, the deity of Jesus Christ, the need for substitutionary atonement, the bodily resurrection or the necessity of personal faith. In all fairness it seems overly harsh to class Seventh-day Adventism with Jehovah's Witnesses, Mormonism, and Christian Science.

There remains reason to question, however, whether Seventh-day Adventism is evangelical in respect to an infallible source of truth in addition to Scripture (Mrs. White's writings), the doctrine of investigative judgment detracting from the completeness of Christ's atonement, and the necessity of law-keeping as a condition of justification.

Are these differences typical of those between Calvinists and Arminians within evangelicalism? If one denies that Adventism is evangelical, does he exclude all who deny eternal security from evangelicalism? These differences, in all three cases, are not characteristic of Arminianism. Arminians do not claim an authoritative body of writings like Mrs. White's. Arminians have not constructed a doctrine like that of the heavenly sanctuary or the investigative judgment compromising the completeness of Christ's work at Calvary. And Arminians do not make any such legalistic use of the commandments as a whole or of the fourth comamndment in particular. The interpretation that takes Adventist doctrine to be Arminian — even in *Questions on Doctrine* — seems too generous.

If Adventism is not ardent evangelicalism or typical cultism then how shall it be classified? The evidence supports Dr. Lindsell's judgment that it is similar to Romanism. Like Romanism Adventism has added to the Scripture a body of tradition it seems reluctant to break. Like Romanism Adventism depreciates the completeness of Christ's work of atonement, and like Romanism Adventism adds to grace the necessity of human works as a condition of salvation. Needless to say, both Adventism and Romanism assert the deity of Christ, His atonement for sinners, and His resurrection from the dead. In other respects their systems may not be analogous except in asserting that the Pope changed the day of worship, but these are highly significant.

The error of Romanism and Adventism resembles that of the Galatians. Adding to the apostolic authority, the Galatians who started with grace were told not to continue in the flesh (Gal. 3:3). They gave ground to those who would pervert the gospel (1:7). But there are not two gospels. Only one message can be identified with the gospel of Christ which Paul had delivered to them. It was not a man's gospel — Paul received it not from man but God (1:11-12). When that gospel was jeopardized by others who believed it but added the Old Testament requirement of circumcision, Paul asked, How can you compel the Gentiles to live like Jews (1:14)?

The Adventists under an influence beyond Scripture (Mrs. White) seem similarly to pervert the gospel by asking Gentiles to live on the sabbath like Jews. Paul underlined the fact that a person is not made righteous due to works of the law, but through faith in Christ. By the works of the law, Paul insisted, no flesh shall be justified (2:16). He then argued if righteousness were through law, Christ died to no purpose (2:21), and that anyone who thought he could be saved by the law, if he did not obey all the laws, was under a curse (3:10). What a tragedy if Adventists today find themselves under that curse when long ago Christ liberated us from it by being made a curse in our place (3:13)! We are not children of the slave woman who represents Mount Sinai (4:24) and the earthly Jerusalem, but we are the children of the free woman and her children.

Although there may be agreement otherwise, Christ's death does not benefit those who depend on circumcision or Sabbath-keeping (5:2). Whoever aims at justification by law-keeping has been dissevered from Christ and has fallen from grace (5:3-4). A bit of yeast raises the whole lump of dough. Believers conduct their lives not according to fleshly cravings, but by the Spirit. But those guided by the Spirit are not under law (5:18). For even the keeping of God's law may be motivated by fleshly desires (6:12-13). With Paul our boast should be in the cross of Christ. What counts is not Saturday-keeping or Sunday-keeping, but a new creation (6:15).

The evangelical's great concern, then, is for individuals in Adventism to be new creatures. Whatever the evaluation of Adventism in general, evangelicals must confront individual Adventists with the one true gospel. If an Adventist will admit that Mrs. White was fallible, that no record in heaven could possibly bring a believer into condemnation, and that works of the law such as Sabbath-keeping are not necessary conditions of salvation, then, other things being equal, he should be acknowledged an evangelical. On the other hand, if the Adventist persists in defending Mrs. White's infallibility, the investigative judgment and the necessity of Old Testament diet and Sabbath-keeping, he chooses for himself the Galatian heresy and places himself under the curse of the law (Gal. 3:10) and of preaching another gospel (Gal. 1:89).

FOOTNOTES

1. Donald Grey Barnhouse, "Are Seventh-day Adventists Christians?" *Eternity*, VII (September, 1956), p. 45.
2. Walter R. Martin, "What Seventh-day Adventists Really Believe," *Eternity*, VII (November, 1956), p. 43.
3. *Questions on Doctrine* (Washington, D. C.: Review and Herald Publishing Association, 1957), p. 9.
4. Walter R. Martin, *The Truth About Seventh-day Adventism* (Grand Rapids: The Zondervan Publishing House, 1960), p. 7.
5. *Ibid.*, p. 10.
6. Harold Lindsell, "What of Seventh-day Adventism?" *Christianity Today*, April 14, 1958, pp. 13, 15.
7. Herbert S. Bird, "Another Look at Adventism," *Christianity Today*, April 28, 1958, p. 16.
8. Bird, *Theology of Seventh-day Adveintism* (Grand Rapids: Wm. B. Eerdmans Publishing Company, 1961), p. 129.
9. Merrill C. Tenney, "Review of the Truth About Seventh-day Adventism," *Eternity*, May, 1960, p. 40.
10. Norman F. Douty, *Another Look at Seventh-day Adventism* (Grand Rapids: Baker Book House, 1962), p. 189.
11. *Ibid.*, p. 188.
12. Anthony A. Hoekema, *The Four Major Cults* (Grand Rapids: Wm. B. Eerdmans Publishing Company, 1963), pp. 377-388.
13. *Ibid.*, p. 389.   14. *Ibid.*, p. 394.   15. *Ibid.*
16. *Ibid.*, p. 400.   17. *Ibid.*, p. 403.
18. *Questions on Doctrine*, p. 11.
19. *Ibid.*, p. 22.   20. *Ibid.*, p. 28.
21. *Bible Reading for the Home Circle* (Washington, D. C.: Review and Herald Publishing Association, 1931), pp. 189-194.
22. Arthur S. Maxwell, *Your Friends the Adventists* (Mountain View, California: Pacific Press Publishing Association, 1960), p. 87.
23. *Questions on Doctrine*, p. 93.
24. Walter R. Martin, *The Truth About Seventh-day Adventism*, pp. 96-97.
25. *Questions on Doctrine*, p. 93.
26. Harold Lindsell, "What of Seventh-day Adventism?" *Christianity Today*, March 31, 1958, p. 7.
27. Walter R. Martin, *The Truth About Seventh-day Adventism*, p. 113.
28. *Ibid.*, pp. 100-104.
29. Ellen G. White, *Testimonies* I, 563, cited by Martin, p. 107. Italics his.
30. *Questions on Doctrine*, pp. 101-102.
31. Arthur S. Maxwell, "What Is a Seventh-day Adventist?" *A Guide to the Religions of America*, ed. Leo Rosten (New York: Simon and Schuster, 1955), p. 133.
32. *Questions on Doctrine*, pp. 11-12.
33. *Ibid.*, p. 515.

34. Norman C. Douty, *op. cit.*, pp. 48-50.
35. *Ibid.*, pp. 52-64; Herbert S. Bird, *Theology of Seventh-day Adventism*, pp. 64-71.
36. *Questions on Doctrine*, pp. 650-652.
37. *Ibid.*, pp. 653-658.   38. *Ibid.*, p. 349.   39. *Ibid.*, p. 350.
40. *Ibid.*, pp. 362-364.
41. Leroy E. Froom, *The Prophetic Faith of Our Fathers* (Washington, D. C.: Review and Herald Publishing Association, 1954), IV, 661.
42. Ellen G. White, *The Great Controversy* (Washington, D. C.: Review and Herald Publishing Association, 1911), p. 420.
43. *Questions on Doctrine*, p. 420.
44. Ellen G. White, *op. cit.*, p. 483.
45. *Ibid.*, p. 482.
46. *Questions on Doctrine*, p. 442.
47. Samuel Zwemer, E. W. Hengstenberg, J. V. Rotherham, and J. Russell Howden in the *Sunday School Times* (Jan. 15, 1927), cited in Walter Martin, *The Truth About Seventh-day Adventism*, pp. 184-188.
48. *Questions on Doctrine*, pp. 397-398.   49. *Ibid.*, p. 400.
50. *Ibid.*, pp. 399-400.   51. *Ibid.*, p. 22.   52. *Ibid.*, p. 66.
53. *Bible Readings for the Home Circle*, 551; 83.
54. Ellen G. White, *Steps to Christ* (Mountain View, California: Pacific Press, 1908), p. 68.
55. *Ibid.*, p. 55.
56. *Questions on Doctrine*, pp. 141-142.   57. *Ibid.*, pp. 65-66.
58. *Bible Readings for the Home Circle*, p. 137.
59. Arthur S. Maxwell, *Your Friends the Adventists*, p. 38.
60. Maxwell, "What Is a Seventh-day Adventist?" p. 136.
61. *Questions on Doctrine*, p. 141.
62. *Ibid.*, pp. 121-134.   63. *Ibid.*, pp. 622-624.
64. Fordyce W. Detamore, *Just What Do You Believe About Your Church?* (Nashville, Tennessee: Southern Publishing Association, n.d.), p. 22-23.
65. *Ibid.*, pp. 32-34.
66. *Questions on Doctrine*, pp. 149-185 (emphasis mine).
67. Herbert S. Bird, *Theology of Seventh-day Adventism*, p. 117.
68. Walter R. Martin, *The Truth About Seventh-day Adventism*, pp. 152-153.
69. Don Phillips, "Taboo: I Was a Seventh-day Adventist," *Power*, Vol. 22, No. 3 (August 16, 1964), p. 6.
70. *Questions on Doctrine*, p. 404 (emphasis mine).
71. Walter R. Martin, *op. cit.*, p. 205.
72. *Ibid.* (emphasis mine).

FOR FURTHER STUDY

ANTHONY A. HOEKEMA, *The Four Major Cults.* (Grand Rapids, Michigan: Wm. B. Eerdmans Publishing Company, 1963). A forceful argument attempting to show that Seventh-day Adventism must be classified as a cult.

HAROLD LINDSELL, "What of Seventh-day Adventism?" *Christianity Today,* Part I (March 31, 1958), p. 6-8; Part II (April 14, 1958), p. 13-15, Presents the view that Seventh-day Adventism is neither cultic nor evangelical, but closest to the legalism of Roman Catholicism.

WALTER R. MARTIN, *The Truth About Seventh-day Adventism.* (Grand Rapids, Michigan: Zondervan Publishing House, 1960). Martin's three years of personal contact and research resulted in this case for accepting Seventh-day Adventism as evangelical.

WALTER R. MARTIN, *The Kingdom of the Cults* (Grand Rapids, Michigan: Zondervan Publishing House, 1965). Against Hoekema and others, Martin writes an appendix replying to those who continue to call Seventh-day Adventism cultic.

Seventh-day Adventists Answer Questions on Doctrine. (Washington, D. C.: Review and Herald Publishing Association, 1957). In response to extensive questioning, this book of more than 700 pages was prepared by a representative group of Seventh-day Adventist leaders, Bible teachers, and editors.

SUGGESTIONS FOR TEACHERS

Good teaching is marked by clarity of purpose. Review the content of this study and attempt to synthesize it in your own mind. This material may best be divided into two sections for two teaching sessions. Put into a few words a statement of objectives for classroom presentation. *Confronting the Cults* differs from some other works on the subject in that its purpose is not primarily negative — refuting false doctrine, but positive — winning cultists to to Christ.

1. Use the lead questions throughout the series to form the major divisions of the teaching sessions. Illustrate the value of these questions in keeping discussion centered on the gospel by moving quickly back to them from irrelevant issues.

2. Anticipate replies Christians may expect to these questions from Seventh-day Adventists. Evaluate the Adventist's position and give specific guidance in answering erroneous beliefs.

3. Build confidence for effective personal witness by helping your group formulate possible approaches and answers. Use simple role playing

situations to involve the group in learning the major doctrines of
Seventh-day Adventists. After the material has been studied allow
several people to take the position of the Adventist in confronting the
evangelical believer. Let others assume the role of evangelicals. Simu-
late a conversation.

SAMPLE LESSON PLAN

SESSION 1

Aim

To guide the class to a knowledge of Seventh-day Adventist teaching on
divine authority, the priority of the gospel and Christ.

To help the class develop skills of witnessing through the use of questions
and proper handling of Scripture.

Approach

Lead a discussion on the attempt to consider Seventh-day Adventism
evangelical.

Outline

I. Divine Authority — Revelation
Question: "Do you base your teachings on revelations other than the
Bible?"

II. The Gospel's Priority
Question: "Is your main business the proclamation of the gospel of
Jesus Christ?"

III. The Doctrine of Christ
Question: "Do you believe that Jesus is the Christ, the eternal Word of
God who has come in the flesh?"

Conclusion and Summation

SESSION 2

Aim

To guide the class to a knowledge of what Seventh-day Adventists believe
about redemption, Christ's resurrection, faith and grace.

To help the class members develop skill in handling the Scriptures as they
contact Seventh-day Adventists.

Confronting the Cults

Approach

Review briefly the three key questions of the previous session.

Outline

I. Redemption
   Question: "Do you believe that Jesus died for your sins?"

II. The Resurrection of Christ
   Question: "Do you believe that Jesus Christ arose from the dead bodily?"

III. Personal Faith
   Question: "Are you personally trusting Jesus Christ as your redeemer and Lord?"

IV. Grace and Law Keeping
   Question: "Do you depend upon some achievements of your own to contribute to justification, or is it only by God's grace through faith?"

Conclusion and Summation